ABeCedarios

Mexican Folk Art ABCs in English and Spanish

Cynthia Weill and K.B. Basseches

Wood Sculptures from **Oaxaca** by
Moisés and Armando Jiménez

the **Armadillo** ❂ el **Armadillo**

the **Buffalo** ✳ el **Búfalo**

the **Coyote** ❋ el **Coyote**

el **Chapulín**

Ch is no longer a letter in the Spanish alphabet, but the sound is still in use.
the grasshopper

the **Dolphin** ✿ el **Delfín**

the **Elephant** ❁ el **Elefante**

the **Flamingo** · el **Flamenco**

the **Gorilla** ◈ el **Gorila**

the **Hippopotamus** ✳ el **Hipopótamo**

the **Iguana** • la **Iguana**

the **Jaguar** ❀ el **Jaguar**

the **Koala** • el **Koala**

the **Lion** ✸ el **León**

la **Ll**ama

Ll is no longer a letter in the Spanish alphabet, but the sound is still in use.
the llama

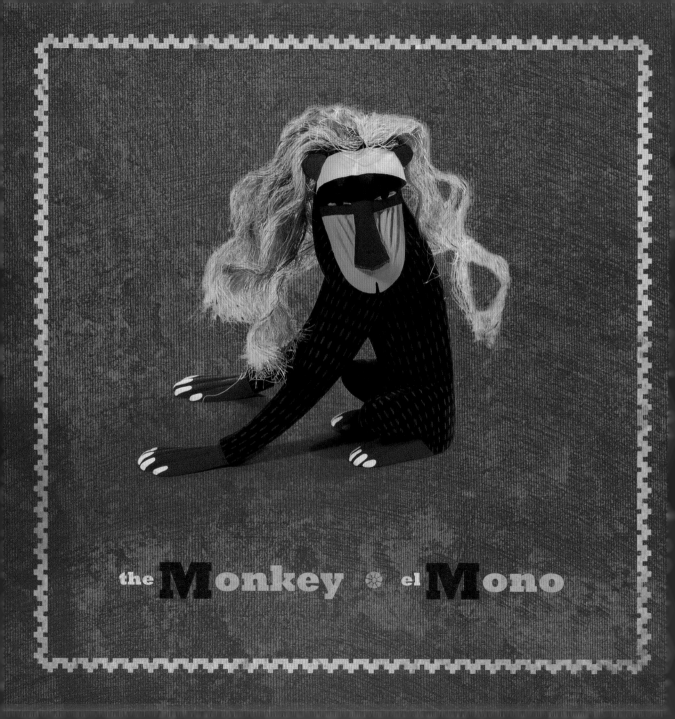

the **Monkey** • el **Mono**

the Nutria ❂ la Nutria

el **Ñu**

Ñ is in the Spanish alphabet only.
the gnu

the **O**celot ❋ el **O**celote

the **Penguin** ❋ el **Pingüino**

the **Quetzal** ❁ el **Quetzal**

the **Rat** ❋ la **Rata**

el zorro

Rr is not a letter in the Spanish alphabet, but the sound is commonly used.
the fox

the **Snake** ✹ la **Serpiente**

the **Turtle** ❖ la **Tortuga**

the **Unicorn** ✹ el **Unicornio**

the **Vicuña** ❀ la **Vicuña**

the **Wapiti** ❀ et **Wapití**

the X ❀ el/la X

This is an undiscovered animal. Can you give it a name starting with the letter X?
Este es un animal desconocido. ¿Puedes darle un nombre que empieza con la letra X?

the **Yak** • el **Yac**

the **Zedonk** ❀ el **Zedonk**

The animals in *ABeCedarios* were handmade by the Jiménez family, who lives in the state of Oaxaca, Mexico. Brothers Armando and Moisés carved the creatures. Their children Alex, Nancy, and Eduardo sanded each one. Then the figures were lovingly painted by their wives, Antonia and Oralia. Armando and Moisés are the grandsons of Manuel Jiménez, founder of the Oaxacan woodcarving tradition. Eighty other families in their town of Arrazola also make woodcarvings.

We have left the letters "ch" and "ll" in *ABeCedarios* even though the Real Academia Española removed them from the Spanish alphabet in 1994. These familiar sounds, along with "rr," are still in use in the living language.

Dedications

To Jean Hebert and Sylvia Lahvis who planted the seeds for this book many years ago. (C.S.W.)
To John Holm for gifts beyond record; and to Adam Edward Basseches-Holm for being himself. (K.B.B.)

Thanks to

Marlene Kurtz, Mari Haas, Talía González, Augusta González, Ann Levine, Hank Baker, Ruth Borgman, the Boucher, Basseches and Holm families, Jeannie Friedman, Inés Greenburger, Will Scanlan, Myriam Chapman, Xochítl Medina, Graeme Sullivan, Hope Leichter, Patricia Velasco, Jossie O'Neill, Ofelía García, Stephanie Owen, Frances and Stephen Weill, Arden Rothstein, Jane Yolen, Jack Bailey, Joseph Seipel, Irene Vazquez, Pamela Taylor, Stephen Carpenter, Alex Bostic, David Burton, and The Bank Street Writers Lab. And a very special thanks goes to Alejandro Jiménez, Raquel Aragón, Mark Basseches, Dr. Richard Toscan and the School of the Arts, Virginia Commonwealth University for travel funds for this project.

Cover and Book Design by

Sergio A. Gómez

Text and photographs copyright © 2007 by Cynthia Weill and K.B. Basseches.
All rights reserved. No part of this book may be reproduced, transmitted, or stored in an information retrieval system in any form or by any means, electronic, mechanical, photocopying, recording, or otherwise, without written permission from the publisher.
Cinco Puntos Press, an imprint of LEE & LOW BOOKS Inc., 95 Madison Avenue, New York, NY 10016, leeandlow.com
Manufactured in South Korea by Mirae-N
First Edition   10 9 8 7 6 5 4 3 2 1
Book production by The Kids at Our House
The text is set in Rockwell Extra Bold and Adobe Caslon Pro
Library of Congress Cataloging-in-Publication Data. Weill, Cynthia. ABeCedarios : Mexican folk art ABCs in English and Spanish / by Cynthia Weill and K.B. Basseches ; animal wood carvings by Moisés and Armando Jiménez. 1st ed. p. cm. HC ISBN 978-1-93369-313-2 PB ISBN 978-1-64379-634-5. Folk art—Mexico. 2. Alphabet in art—Juvenile literature. 3. Alphabet books—Juvenile literature. I. Basseches, K. B. II. Jiménez., Moisés. III. Jiménez., Armando. IV. Title. NK844.W45 2007 745.0972—dc22 2007019441

MIX
Paper from responsible sources
FSC® C010275